Artificial Intelligence for beguinners

"Exploring the limits and opportunities of artificial intelligence in the world"

By Daniel Huston

IV. _Ethical and Social Implications of AI_

V.   _Future of AI_

VI.   _Conclusion A. Recap of key points_

Introduction

As we enter the era of technological advancement and innovation, Artificial Intelligence (AI) has become one of the most talked-about and significant developments in recent years. With the vast potential to transform industries, improve our lives, and address some of the world's biggest challenges, AI has captured the imagination of experts, policymakers, and the general public alike.

But despite its growing prominence, AI can still seem complex and confusing to many. The language used to describe AI is often technical and academic, making it difficult for people to fully understand the capabilities and limitations of this emerging technology.

This is where this book comes in. "Artificial Intelligence for beguinners" takes a clear, concise, and accessible approach to the subject, providing a comprehensive overview of AI for those with little or no background in the field. Through easy-to-follow explanations and real-world examples, the author demystifies the complex concepts behind AI, making it accessible and understandable to everyone.

Artificial Intelligence (AI) is a branch of computer science that aims to create intelligent machines that can perform tasks that would normally require human intelligence, such as visual perception, speech recognition, decision-making, and language translation. AI has been a topic of research and development since the 1950s, and recent advancements in technology have made it possible to achieve significant breakthroughs in the field.

The history of AI can be traced back to the invention of computers. The earliest AI programs were developed in the 1950s and 1960s and were designed to perform simple mathematical calculations. In 1956, John McCarthy, Marvin Minsky, Nathaniel Rochester, and Claude Shannon organized the Dartmouth Conference, which is widely considered the birthplace of AI as a field of research.

One of the key goals of AI research is to create systems that can perform tasks that are typically performed by humans, such as speech recognition and understanding, problem solving, decision making, and learning. AI systems can be divided into two broad categories: rule-based systems and machine learning systems. Rule-based systems use a set of pre-defined rules to make decisions, while machine learning systems use algorithms to learn from data and make decisions based on that data.

One of the most well-known applications of AI is natural language processing (NLP). NLP is the use of computers to process, understand, and generate human language. NLP systems are used in a variety of applications, including language translation, sentiment analysis, and speech recognition. For example, Apple's Siri and Amazon's Alexa are voice-controlled AI assistants that use NLP to understand and respond to user requests.

Another important area of AI research is computer vision, which is the ability of computers to interpret and understand visual information. Computer vision systems can be used in a variety of applications, including object recognition, face recognition, and image analysis. For example, computer vision systems are used in self-driving cars to detect and respond to road conditions, traffic signals, and other vehicles.

Another application of AI is expert systems, which are designed to perform tasks that would normally require human expertise. Expert systems are used in a variety of fields, including medicine, finance, and law. For example, a medical expert system might be used to diagnose a disease based on a patient's symptoms, while a financial expert system might be used to recommend investment strategies based on market trends.

One of the most exciting developments in AI is the rise of deep learning, a subfield of machine learning that is based on artificial neural networks. Deep learning algorithms use multiple layers of neural networks to analyze and interpret data, allowing them to learn complex patterns and make predictions with high accuracy. Deep learning algorithms are used in a variety of applications, including image recognition, speech recognition, and natural language processing.

Despite the many exciting developments in AI, there are also a number of challenges that must be addressed before AI can reach its full potential. One of the biggest challenges is ensuring that AI systems are transparent and interpretable, so that their decisions can be understood and trusted. Another challenge is ensuring that AI systems are secure and protected against hacking and malicious use. In conclusion, AI is a rapidly growing field that has the potential to revolutionize the way we live and work. From speech recognition and natural language processing to computer vision and expert systems, AI is changing the way we interact with technology and opening up new avenues of research and development. While there are still many challenges to overcome, the future of AI is bright and holds great promise for improving our lives and solving some of the world's biggest problems. While there are still many challenges to overcome, the future of AI is bright and holds great

Another area of AI research is computer vision, which is the ability of computers to interpret and understand visual information. Computer vision systems can be used in a variety of applications, including object recognition, face recognition, and image analysis. For example, computer vision systems are used in self-driving cars to detect and respond to road conditions, traffic signals, and other vehicles.

Another application of AI is expert systems, which are designed to perform tasks that would normally require human expertise. Expert systems are used in a variety of fields, including medicine, finance, and law. For example, a medical expert system might be used to diagnose a disease based on a patient's symptoms, while a financial expert system might be used to recommend investment strategies based on market trends.

One of the most exciting developments in AI is the rise of deep learning, a subfield of machine learning that is based on artificial neural networks. Deep learning algorithms use multiple layers of neural networks to analyze and interpret data, allowing them to learn complex patterns and make predictions with high accuracy. Deep learning algorithms are used in a variety of applications, including image recognition, speech recognition, and natural language processing.

Despite the many advancements in AI, there are also a number of challenges that must be addressed before AI can reach its full potential. One of the biggest challenges is ensuring that AI systems are transparent and interpretable, so that their decisions can be understood and trusted. Another challenge is ensuring that AI systems are secure and protected against hacking and malicious use.

In conclusion, AI is a rapidly growing field that has the potential to revolutionize the way we live and work. From speech recognition and natural language processing to computer vision and expert systems, AI is changing the way we interact with technology and opening up new avenues of research and development. While there are still many challenges to overcome, the future of AI is bright and holds great promise for improving our lives and solving some of the world's biggest problems.

I

Introduction

Definition of Artificial Intelligence

Artificial Intelligence (AI) is a rapidly growing field that encompasses various disciplines of computer science, mathematics, psychology, and engineering. It involves the creation of computer systems that can perform tasks that would normally require human intelligence to complete. This can include tasks such as pattern recognition, decision-making, speech recognition, and language translation, among others.

AI can be divided into two main categories: narrow or weak AI, and strong or general AI. Narrow AI, also known as domain-specific AI, is designed to perform a specific task, such as facial recognition or playing a game of chess. These AI systems are trained on large amounts of data and use algorithms to identify patterns and make predictions based on that data. They are limited by their programming and can only perform the specific task for which they were designed.

Strong AI, on the other hand, is designed to be capable of performing any intellectual task that a human can. This type of AI is still in its infancy and is the subject of much research and development. The ultimate goal of strong AI is to create a system that is capable of learning, reasoning, and self-correction, just like a human being.

The development of AI has been driven by advancements in computing power, the availability of large amounts of data, and the development of sophisticated algorithms. One of the most important algorithms in AI is known as deep learning, which is a type of machine learning that is modeled after the structure and function of the human brain. Deep learning algorithms are used to process large amounts of data and identify patterns, allowing AI systems to improve their performance over time.

One of the primary benefits of AI is that it has the potential to automate many tasks that are currently performed by humans. This can lead to increased efficiency and productivity, as well as the ability to perform tasks that are too dangerous or difficult for humans to perform. For example, AI systems can be used to perform surgery with greater precision and accuracy than a human surgeon, or to search for oil and gas reserves in areas that are difficult for humans to reach.

However, the development of AI also raises important ethical and societal questions. For example, as AI systems become more capable, there is a risk that they may replace human workers, leading to job loss and economic disruption. Additionally, AI systems may make decisions that have significant consequences for individuals or society, raising concerns about accountability and bias. There are also concerns about the use of AI in military applications, as well as the potential for AI systems to be used for malicious purposes, such as cyber attacks or the spread of false information.

To address these concerns, it is important that the development of AI be guided by a set of ethical principles and that there be ongoing dialogue between researchers, policymakers, and the public about the future of AI and its impact on society. There is also a growing movement to promote responsible AI practices, such as the use of transparent algorithms and the development of systems that can explain their decisions.

In conclusion, Artificial Intelligence is a rapidly evolving field that has the potential to transform the way we live and work. While it presents both opportunities and challenges, it is important that we approach the development of AI with a clear understanding of its capabilities and limitations, and with a commitment to ethical and responsible practices. By doing so, we can ensure that AI is used to enhance and enrich human life, rather than threatening it

Overview of AI applications and technologies

Artificial Intelligence (AI) has seen tremendous growth and progress in recent years and has become an increasingly important technology for businesses and organizations across industries. AI is used to automate tasks that would normally require human intelligence, such as decision-making, language translation, speech recognition, and image recognition, among others. This has led to a wide range of AI applications and technologies that are transforming the way we live and work.

One of the most common applications of AI is in the field of customer service. AI-powered chatbots are increasingly being used to interact with customers, providing quick and convenient answers to their questions and concerns. These chatbots use natural language processing (NLP) algorithms to understand and respond to customer inquiries, and they can be trained to handle a wide range of customer service scenarios.

Another important area of AI application is in the field of marketing and sales. AI-powered systems are being used to analyze customer data and predict customer behavior, allowing businesses to create more personalized and effective marketing campaigns. AI is also being used to automate lead generation, qualification, and scoring processes, helping businesses to identify the most promising sales leads and prioritize their follow-up efforts.

In the field of healthcare, AI is being used to improve patient outcomes and reduce costs. AI algorithms are being used to analyze medical images, such as X-rays and MRIs, to identify signs of disease and provide doctors with more accurate diagnoses. AI is also being used to analyze large amounts of patient data to identify patterns and predict future health outcomes, allowing healthcare providers to intervene earlier and provide more effective treatments.

AI is also having a significant impact on the financial services industry. AI algorithms are being used to detect fraud and prevent financial crimes, such as money laundering and identity theft. AI is also being used to automate back-office processes, such as loan underwriting and risk management, improving efficiency and reducing costs.

In the field of transportation and logistics, AI is being used to optimize delivery routes, reduce fuel consumption, and improve the safety of vehicles. AI algorithms are being used to analyze data from sensors and cameras in real-time, providing drivers with information about traffic conditions and potential hazards on the road.

AI is also being used in the field of cybersecurity to detect and prevent cyber attacks. AI algorithms are used to analyze network data in real-time, identify unusual activity, and respond to threats before they cause damage. AI is also being used to automate threat hunting, allowing security teams to more effectively identify and respond to threats.

There are several key technologies that are driving the development of AI applications, including machine learning, deep learning, and computer vision. Machine learning involves the use of algorithms that can learn from data and improve their performance over time. Deep learning is a type of machine learning that is modeled after the structure and function of the human brain, allowing AI systems to process large amounts of data and identify patterns. Computer vision is a field of AI that focuses on enabling computers to interpret and understand visual information, such as images and videos.

In addition to these technologies, there is also a growing interest in the development of explainable AI (XAI) systems, which are designed to provide clear and understandable explanations for their decisions. XAI is important for building trust in AI systems and ensuring that they are used ethically and responsibly.

In conclusion, AI is a rapidly evolving technology that is transforming many industries and improving the way we live and work. From customer service and marketing to healthcare and transportation, AI is being used to automate tasks, improve efficiency, and provide new insights and capabilities. The development of AI is being driven by advances in machine learning, deep learning, computer vision, and explainable AI, and it is an exciting time for the field as

Importance of AI in today's world

Artificial Intelligence (AI) has become one of the most important and rapidly growing technologies in the world today. Its impact can be felt across a wide range of industries and sectors, from healthcare and finance to transportation and retail. AI has the potential to revolutionize the way we live and work, improving efficiency, productivity, and quality of life.

One of the main advantages of AI is its ability to automate tasks that would normally require human intelligence. This has significant implications for productivity, as AI systems can perform tasks faster and more accurately than humans, freeing up time for more creative and strategic work. For example, in the financial services industry, AI is being used to automate loan underwriting and risk management processes, allowing banks to make more informed decisions and improve the speed and efficiency of these processes.

AI is also having a major impact on the healthcare industry. AI algorithms are being used to analyze medical images, such as X-rays and MRIs, to identify signs of disease and provide doctors with more accurate diagnoses. AI is also being used to analyze large amounts of patient data to identify patterns and predict future health outcomes, allowing healthcare providers to intervene earlier and provide more effective treatments.

Another important benefit of AI is its ability to process and analyze large amounts of data in real-time. This allows organizations to gain new insights into their operations and make more informed decisions. For example, in the retail industry, AI is being used to analyze customer data and predict customer behavior, allowing retailers to create more personalized and effective marketing campaigns. AI is also being used to optimize delivery routes and reduce fuel consumption in the transportation industry, improving efficiency and reducing costs.

In addition to its benefits for business and industry, AI is also having a significant impact on our daily lives. AI-powered virtual assistants, such as Siri and Alexa, are becoming increasingly popular, allowing people to control their homes and access information more easily. AI is also being used to improve accessibility for people with disabilities, such as text-to-speech technology and facial recognition systems.

The importance of AI in today's world is also being recognized by governments and international organizations. Many countries are investing in AI research and development, recognizing the potential of this technology to drive economic growth and create new jobs. The European Union, for example, has launched the European AI Alliance

II

Understanding AI

Types of AI

Artificial Intelligence (AI) is a rapidly growing field that has the potential to revolutionize the way we live and work. There are various types of AI, each with its own unique capabilities and applications. In this article, we will explore the different types of AI and their uses.

Reactive Machines: Reactive machines are the simplest type of AI and are designed to perform a specific task in real-time. They have no memory or past experiences and only respond to the current situation. Examples of reactive machines include Deep Blue, the chess-playing computer that defeated Garry Kasparov in 1997, and self-driving cars that use sensors and algorithms to navigate roads in real-time.

Limited Memory: Limited memory AI systems have a short-term memory that allows them to use past experiences to inform their current actions. For example, a self-driving car that uses limited memory AI would be able to remember the location of road signs and traffic lights, and use this information to make better driving decisions in the future.

Theory of Mind: Theory of mind AI systems are designed to understand and model the beliefs, intentions, and emotions of other entities. This type of AI is still in its early stages of development and is considered a form of general or strong AI.

Self-Aware: Self-aware AI systems are capable of introspection and self-awareness. This type of AI is still purely theoretical and has not yet been developed in a practical sense.

Narrow or Weak AI: Narrow AI is designed to perform a specific task and is limited to that task. This type of AI is currently the most common and is used in a variety of applications, such as speech recognition, image classification, and natural language processing.

General or Strong AI: General AI, also known as strong AI, is capable of performing any intellectual task that a human can. This type of AI is still in its early stages of development and is considered a long-term goal of the AI research community.

Machine Learning: Machine learning is a type of artificial intelligence that allows machines to learn from data and improve their performance over time. There are three main types of machine learning algorithms: supervised learning, unsupervised learning, and reinforcement learning.

Deep Learning: Deep learning is a type of machine learning that uses deep neural networks to process and analyze large amounts of data. Deep learning algorithms have been shown to be highly effective in a variety of applications, such as image recognition, natural language processing, and speech recognition.

Natural Language Processing (NLP): NLP is a type of AI that focuses on the processing and analysis of human language. NLP algorithms are used in a variety of applications, such as chatbots, language translation systems, and sentiment analysis tools.

Robotics: Robotics is a type of AI that focuses on the design and development of robots. Robotics AI systems are used in a variety of applications, such as manufacturing, healthcare, and military.

Computer Vision: Computer vision is a type of AI that focuses on the interpretation and understanding of visual information. Computer vision algorithms are used in a variety of applications, such as image recognition, object detection, and facial recognition.

In conclusion, AI is a rapidly growing field that encompasses a wide range of technologies and applications. From reactive machines to self-aware AI, each type of AI has its own unique capabilities and uses. As AI continues to advance, it is likely that we will see new types of AI emerge and become increasingly important in our lives.

How AI works

Artificial Intelligence (AI) has rapidly grown into a highly influential and powerful field, with applications in numerous industries and daily life.

At its core, AI is about developing computer systems that can   perform tasks that normally require human intelligence, such as recognizing speech, making decisions, and understanding natural language. But how exactly does AI work? In this article, we will explore the fundamental concepts and processes behind AI.

1.   Algorithms

AI algorithms are the foundation of AI systems, and they are designed to perform specific tasks such as decision making, pattern recognition, and prediction. There are numerous types of AI algorithms, including supervised learning, unsupervised learning, reinforcement learning, and deep learning, each of which are used for different purposes.

2.   Data

Data is the fuel that powers AI systems. The more data an AI system has, the more accurate and effective it can be. Data can come from a variety of sources, including databases, images, videos, and audio files. AI algorithms use this data to learn and make predictions.

3.   Neural Networks

Neural networks are a type of AI algorithm that are modeled after the structure and function of the human brain. Neural networks consist of interconnected nodes, each of which can perform a specific task, such as recognizing patterns or making predictions. By connecting multiple nodes, neural networks can perform complex tasks, such as recognizing speech or identifying objects in an image.

4.   Training

Training is the process of teaching an AI system to perform a specific task, such as recognizing speech or making decisions. During the training process, an AI system is fed a large amount of data and uses that data to learn and make predictions. The system is then evaluated on its performance and any errors or inaccuracies are corrected, allowing it to learn and improve over time.

5.   Deployment

Once an AI system has been trained, it is ready to be deployed in a real-world environment. During deployment, the AI system uses the knowledge and experience gained during the training process to perform the specific task it was designed for, such as recognizing speech or making decisions.

6.   Maintenance and Updating

AI systems are not static, and they need to be maintained and updated regularly to ensure they continue to perform at optimal levels. This may involve updating the algorithms, adding new data, or adjusting the parameters of the system. Regular maintenance and updating is critical for ensuring the accuracy and reliability of AI systems over time.

In conclusion, AI is a complex and multi-faceted field that involves the development of algorithms, the use of data, and the deployment of AI systems in real-world environments. By understanding the fundamental concepts and processes behind AI, we can better appreciate its power and potential, as well as its limitations and challenges. As AI continues to grow and evolve, it will undoubtedly play an increasingly important role in our daily lives and the global economy.

How to use artificial intelligence

Artificial Intelligence (AI) has been a buzzword in the technology industry for some time now. It is a branch of computer science that deals with the creation of intelligent machines that can perform tasks without explicit instructions. AI has the potential to revolutionize the way we live, work, and interact with technology.

Here's how you can use Artificial Intelligence:

1.   Machine learning: Machine learning is a subset of AI that involves training computers to recognize patterns in data and make predictions based on that data. This can be used in a variety of applications, including image recognition, speech recognition, and natural language processing.

2.   Computer vision: Computer vision is a field of AI that focuses on enabling computers to understand and interpret visual data. This can be used in applications such as image classification, object detection, and face recognition.

3.   Natural language processing (NLP): NLP is a field of AI that deals with the interactions between computers and humans using natural language. This can be used in applications such as sentiment analysis, text classification, and language translation.

4.   Robotics: AI can be used to control and program robots to perform a wide range of tasks. This can be used in industries such as manufacturing, healthcare, and retail.

5. Predictive analytics: Predictive analytics is a branch of AI that uses data, statistical algorithms, and machine learning techniques to identify the likelihood of future outcomes based on historical data. This can be used in a variety of applications, including marketing, finance, and healthcare.

6. Customer service: AI can be used to provide automated customer service, such as chatbots, that can handle simple inquiries and provide information to customers.

7. Personalization: AI can be used to provide personalized experiences for users, such as personalized recommendations, advertisements, and content.

8. Fraud detection: AI can be used to detect fraudulent activities, such as credit card fraud, by analyzing patterns in data and identifying unusual behavior.

9. Healthcare: AI has the potential to revolutionize the healthcare industry by enabling healthcare professionals to make more accurate diagnoses, develop personalized treatment plans, and improve patient outcomes.

10. Supply chain management: AI can be used to optimize supply chain management by analyzing

data, predicting demand, and optimizing the movement of goods and resources.

To get started with AI, it is important to have a good understanding of its concepts and techniques. You can learn about AI by taking online courses, reading books, and attending conferences. It is also important to have experience with programming and data analysis, as these are essential skills for working with AI.

Once you have a solid understanding of AI, you can start building your own AI applications using open-source tools and frameworks, such as TensorFlow, PyTorch, and scikit-learn. You can also participate in AI hackathons and Kaggle competitions to gain hands-on experience and learn from others in the AI community.

In conclusion, AI has the potential to revolutionize the way we live, work, and interact with technology. By learning about AI and its applications, and by gaining hands-on experience building AI applications, you can position yourself to take advantage of the many opportunities that AI has to offer.

Machine learning and deep learning

Machine learning (ML) and deep learning (DL) are two closely related branches of artificial intelligence (AI) that are changing the way we live and work. These technologies are used to develop computer systems that can learn and make predictions without being explicitly programmed. In this article, we will explore what machine learning and deep learning are, how they work, and their applications in various industries.

1.   Machine Learning

Machine learning is a type of artificial intelligence that allows computer systems to learn and make predictions based on data. Machine learning algorithms use statistical models and algorithms to analyze and make predictions based on data. There are three main types of machine learning: supervised learning, unsupervised learning, and reinforcement learning.

•   Supervised learning: In supervised learning, an algorithm is trained on a labeled dataset, meaning the data is already labeled with the correct answer. The algorithm uses this information to learn and make predictions on new, unseen data.

•   Unsupervised learning: In unsupervised learning, the algorithm is not provided with labeled data and must find patterns and relationships in the data on its own. This type of machine learning is often used for clustering, where data is grouped based on similar characteristics.

• Reinforcement learning: Reinforcement learning is a type of machine learning where an algorithm learns through trial and error, receiving rewards or penalties for certain actions. This type of learning is often used for applications such as robotics, gaming, and decision making.

2. Deep Learning

Deep learning is a type of machine learning that uses artificial neural networks, which are designed to mimic the structure and function of the human brain. These neural networks can process large amounts of data and make predictions based on that data. There are three main types of deep learning: convolutional neural networks, recurrent neural networks, and generative adversarial networks.

• Convolutional neural networks (CNNs): CNNs are used for image and video recognition and processing. They are designed to identify patterns and objects in images and videos, making them ideal for applications such as computer vision and image classification.

• Recurrent neural networks (RNNs): RNNs are used for sequence data, such as text and speech. They are designed to process data in a sequential manner, allowing them to analyze and make predictions based on time-series data.

• Generative adversarial networks (GANs): GANs are used for generative tasks, such as creating new images or music. They consist of two neural networks, a generator and a discriminator, that work together to generate new data.

3. Applications of Machine Learning and Deep Learning

Machine learning and deep learning have numerous applications in various industries, including healthcare, finance, transportation, and entertainment. Some of the most common applications include:

• Healthcare: Machine learning and deep learning are used to analyze and make predictions based on medical images, such as X-rays and MRI scans, to assist doctors in diagnosis and treatment.

• Finance: Machine learning and deep learning are used to analyze financial data and make predictions about market trends and stock prices.

This information can be used to inform investment decisions and reduce risk.

• Transportation: Machine learning and deep learning are used to analyze traffic patterns and make predictions about traffic flow and congestion, allowing cities to optimize their transportation systems.

• Entertainment: Machine learning and deep learning are used to create and improve virtual assistants, chatbots, and personalized recommendations in areas such as music, movies, and video games.

In conclusion, machine learning and deep learning are rapidly growing fields that are changing the way we live and work. These technologies are used to develop computer systems that can learn and make predictions based on data.

Machine learning and deep learning

Machine learning (ML) and deep learning (DL) are two important subfields of artificial intelligence (AI) that have garnered significant attention in recent years. ML is a type of AI that allows machines to learn from data and improve their performance over time, without being explicitly programmed. DL, on the other hand, is a type of machine learning that uses deep neural networks to process and analyze large amounts of data.

Machine learning algorithms can be broadly classified into three categories: supervised learning, unsupervised learning, and reinforcement learning. In supervised learning, the machine is trained on a labeled dataset, where the correct output is known in advance. The machine uses this training data to learn a function that maps inputs to outputs, and this function can then be applied to new, unseen data. Supervised learning is commonly used in applications such as image classification and spam filtering.

Unsupervised learning, on the other hand, involves training the machine on an unlabeled dataset, where the correct output is unknown. The goal of unsupervised learning is to identify patterns and structure in the data, without any prior knowledge of what the output should be. Unsupervised learning algorithms are commonly used in applications such as dimensionality reduction and clustering.

Reinforcement learning involves training the machine through trial and error, by providing it with a reward signal that indicates whether its actions are good or bad. Reinforcement learning algorithms are commonly used in applications such as robotics and game playing.

Deep learning is a type of machine learning that uses deep neural networks to process and analyze large amounts of data. Deep neural networks consist of multiple layers of interconnected nodes, and are designed to automatically extract and learn features from the data. Unlike traditional machine learning algorithms, which rely on hand-crafted features, deep learning algorithms learn the features directly from the data, making them highly effective in applications such as image recognition and natural language processing.

Deep learning algorithms are particularly well-suited for tasks that involve large amounts of unstructured data, such as images and text. The ability of deep neural networks to automatically extract and learn features from the data has made them highly effective in a variety of applications, including image recognition, speech recognition, natural language processing, and autonomous driving.

One of the key advantages of deep learning is that it is highly scalable. As more data becomes available, deep learning algorithms can continue to learn and improve, making them highly effective in real-world applications. Additionally, deep learning algorithms are highly flexible and can be applied to a wide range of tasks, making them a powerful tool for solving complex problems.

In conclusion, ML and DL are two important subfields of AI that have the potential to transform a wide range of industries. ML provides the ability to train machines to learn from data and improve their performance over time, while DL allows machines to process and analyze large amounts of data in a highly effective and scalable manner. As AI continues to advance, it is likely that we will see more and more applications of ML and DL in the years to come.

Natural language processing

Natural language processing (NLP) is an interdisciplinary field of computer science and linguistics concerned with the interactions between computers and human (natural) languages. The goal of NLP is to develop algorithms and models that enable computers to understand, interpret, generate, and even learn from human language.

NLP has become increasingly important in recent years, as the amount of text data generated by people has grown rapidly, making it challenging for humans to process and understand all this information. With the help of NLP, computers can help humans to extract meaningful insights from this data, making it easier to make informed decisions.

One of the key challenges in NLP is the complexity of human language. Unlike computer programming languages, natural language is often ambiguous, context-dependent, and culturally specific. This means that NLP algorithms need to be able to handle these complexities, which requires sophisticated mathematical models and algorithms.

Another challenge in NLP is the difficulty in defining what it means for a computer to "understand" human language. Unlike computer programming languages, which have well-defined syntax and semantics, human language is more subjective and open to interpretation. As a result, NLP researchers often use a variety of metrics and benchmarks to evaluate the performance of NLP models, including accuracy, precision, recall, and F1 score.

One of the key applications of NLP is information extraction, which involves automatically extracting information from text data. This can include extracting named entities (such as people, organizations, and locations), relationships between entities, and semantic roles (such as subject and object). Information extraction is used in a variety of domains, including news articles, legal documents, and social media posts.

Another important application of NLP is sentiment analysis, which involves determining the sentiment or emotion expressed in text. This can be used to determine the public opinion of a particular product, brand, or political figure, or to analyze the sentiment of customer feedback or reviews.

Machine translation is another important application of NLP. With the help of NLP algorithms, computers can translate text from one language to another, making it easier for people to communicate with each other across language barriers. While machine translation has come a long way in recent years, it still has its limitations and there is much room for improvement.

In addition to these applications, NLP is also used in a variety of other areas, including text summarization, question answering, dialogue systems, and text classification.

There are many tools and libraries available for NLP, including NLTK, spaCy, Gensim, and OpenNLP. These tools provide pre-trained models and algorithms for a variety of NLP tasks, making it easier for researchers and developers to get started with NLP.

Despite the many advances in NLP in recent years, there is still much work to be done. NLP researchers are constantly working to improve existing models and algorithms, and to develop new ones to address the challenges of human language. Additionally, NLP has the potential to have a significant impact on society, and researchers are exploring new applications for NLP that could change the way we live and work.

In conclusion, natural language processing is a rapidly growing field with a wide range of applications. With the help of NLP algorithms, computers can help humans to extract meaningful insights from text data, making it easier to make informed decisions. While there are still many challenges to be addressed in NLP, the potential for impact is huge, and NLP researchers are working hard to make this a reality.

Computer vision

Computer vision is a rapidly growing field of computer science that focuses on enabling computers to interpret and understand visual information from the world in the same way that humans do. It involves the development of algorithms and models that can process images and videos to extract meaningful information, such as object recognition, image segmentation, and motion analysis.

The goal of computer vision is to give computers the ability to understand and interpret visual information, making it possible for them to perform tasks that typically require human-level perception and understanding. This includes tasks such as recognizing objects in images, detecting faces in photos, tracking moving objects in videos, and more.

Computer vision is used in a wide range of applications, including self-driving cars, facial recognition, medical imaging, and surveillance systems. For example, self-driving cars rely on computer vision to interpret visual information from cameras and sensors to make decisions about how to navigate the road. In the medical field, computer vision is used to process and analyze medical images, such as X-rays and MRI scans, to help diagnose diseases and conditions. And in surveillance systems, computer vision is used to analyze video footage to detect potential security threats and identify criminal activities.

The development of computer vision has been greatly helped by the availability of large amounts of data, the increase in computational power, and the advancements in deep learning algorithms. Deep learning algorithms, in particular, have allowed computer vision models to improve significantly in recent years, with many achieving human-level performance on tasks such as object recognition and image classification.

However, there are still many challenges in computer vision that need to be addressed. One of the biggest challenges is developing algorithms that can work well in real-world conditions, such as varying lighting and weather conditions, and dealing with complex and cluttered backgrounds. Another challenge is to make computer vision systems more robust and reliable, especially in situations where a single mistake can have serious consequences, such as self-driving cars or medical imaging.

Another challenge in computer vision is privacy. With the increasing use of computer vision in surveillance and facial recognition systems, there is a growing concern about the potential misuse of this technology to invade people's privacy. This has led to increased scrutiny and regulations surrounding the use of computer vision, making it important for researchers and developers to ensure that these systems are used in ethical and responsible ways.

In conclusion, computer vision is a rapidly growing field with a wide range of applications. With the help of computer vision algorithms, computers can process and analyze vast amounts of visual data, making it easier for humans to make informed decisions based on this information. While there are still many challenges to be addressed in computer vision, the potential for impact is huge, and researchers and developers are working hard to make this a reality.

III

Developing AI Solutions

Problem definition

Developing AI solutions requires a well-defined problem definition, as this sets the foundation for the entire AI project. A clear understanding of the problem to be solved is crucial for designing and implementing effective AI solutions.

The problem definition process involves a deep understanding of the problem at hand and the goals to be achieved. This requires a thorough analysis of the problem domain and the collection of relevant data and information. The problem definition should also take into consideration the stakeholders involved, such as customers, end-users, and the business, and their specific requirements and expectations.

Once the problem is defined, the next step is to determine the feasibility of the solution. This involves evaluating the available resources, such as data, computational power, and human expertise, and determining if they are sufficient to develop an AI solution. It is also important to consider the technical limitations of AI and if they can be overcome to solve the problem.

The problem definition process also involves defining the scope of the project, which is essential for setting realistic goals and expectations. This includes determining the boundaries of the project, such as the scope of the data to be used, the timeline for the project, and the budget. The scope should also take into account the risk management plan, which is an important aspect of AI projects and helps to minimize potential risks and ensure the success of the project.

In addition, the problem definition should also outline the desired outcome of the AI solution. This involves defining the metrics and KPIs that will be used to evaluate the success of the solution, as well as the expected impact on the stakeholders. The desired outcome should be realistic, measurable, and aligned with the goals of the project.

Finally, the problem definition process should include a plan for validating the AI solution. This includes setting up experiments and tests to ensure that the solution meets the desired outcome and performs as expected. The validation process should also include a plan for continuous improvement, as AI solutions are never final and can always be improved upon.

In conclusion, developing an AI solution requires a well-defined problem definition, which sets the foundation for the entire project. A clear understanding of the problem to be solved and the desired outcome, combined with an assessment of feasibility and a plan for validation, are all crucial components of a successful AI project.

Data collection and preparation

Data collection and preparation are critical stages in the process of developing AI solutions. The quality of the data used in AI projects directly impacts the performance of the solution, so it is essential to carefully consider the data that is collected and how it is prepared.

The first step in data collection is to identify the data sources that will be used for the AI solution. This could include internal data sources, such as databases or spreadsheets, or external sources, such as publicly available datasets or third-party APIs. The data sources should be carefully evaluated to ensure that they are reliable and relevant to the problem being solved.

Once the data sources have been identified, the next step is to collect the data. This can be done through various methods, such as web scraping, data extraction from APIs, or manual data entry. It is important to consider the size and complexity of the data, as well as the methods used to collect it, as this can impact the time and resources required to collect the data.

Once the data has been collected, the next step is to prepare it for use in the AI solution. This involves a number of tasks, such as cleaning the data to remove any errors or inconsistencies, transforming the data into a format that is suitable for use in the AI solution, and splitting the data into training and test sets.

Data preparation also involves feature engineering, which is the process of creating new features from existing data to improve the performance of the AI solution. This could include combining multiple features, creating new features based on existing data, or removing irrelevant features. Feature engineering is a critical stage in data preparation and can greatly impact the performance of the AI solution.

Another important aspect of data preparation is data normalization, which is the process of transforming the data into a standard format. This is important as AI algorithms are sensitive to the scale of the data, so normalizing the data helps to ensure that the algorithms are trained on data that is consistent and comparable.

Data preparation also involves data augmentation, which is the process of artificially increasing the size of the dataset. This is done by applying various transformations to the data, such as rotating, flipping, or scaling the images, to increase the diversity of the data and improve the robustness of the AI solution.

In conclusion, data collection and preparation are critical stages in the process of developing AI solutions. The quality of the data used in AI projects directly impacts the performance of the solution, so it is essential to carefully consider the data that is collected and how it is prepared. The data preparation process involves cleaning the data, transforming it into a suitable format, normalizing it, and augmenting it to increase its size and diversity.

Model selection and training

Model selection and training are two of the most important stages in the process of developing AI solutions. The choice of model and the way it is trained have a significant impact on the performance of the solution, so it is crucial to carefully consider these aspects of the AI project.

Model selection involves choosing the most appropriate algorithm for the problem being solved. There are many different AI algorithms to choose from, each with its own strengths and weaknesses, so it is important to understand the problem domain and the goals of the project to determine which algorithm is best suited. Some of the most commonly used AI algorithms include decision trees, neural networks, support vector machines, and k-nearest neighbors.

Once the model has been selected, the next step is to train it. The process of training an AI model involves providing it with data and adjusting its parameters so that it can make accurate predictions. This is done by dividing the data into two parts: a training set and a test set. The model is trained on the training set and its performance is evaluated on the test set. This process is repeated until the model reaches a level of performance that is satisfactory for the problem being solved.

The training process involves adjusting the model's parameters to minimize the difference between its predictions and the actual values in the training data. This is done using various optimization algorithms, such as gradient descent or stochastic gradient descent. The optimization process continues until the model reaches a local minimum in the error function, which represents the difference between its predictions and the actual values.

Hyperparameter tuning is another important aspect of model training. Hyperparameters are parameters that are not learned by the model during training, but are set by the user. Examples of hyperparameters include the learning rate, the number of hidden layers in a neural network, or the regularization strength. Hyperparameter tuning involves selecting the optimal values for the hyperparameters to improve the performance of the model.

Overfitting is a common issue in model training and occurs when the model becomes too complex and begins to fit the training data too closely, resulting in poor performance on new, unseen data. To prevent overfitting, regularization techniques can be used, such as L1 or L2 regularization. Regularization adds a penalty to the error function that discourages the model from fitting the training data too closely.

Ensemble learning is another technique that can be used to improve the performance of AI models. Ensemble learning involves combining the predictions of multiple models to produce a more accurate prediction. This can be done by combining the predictions of different models, such as different algorithms or different hyperparameter settings, or by combining the predictions of different instances of the same model.

In conclusion, model selection and training are two of the most important stages in the process of developing AI solutions. The choice of model and the way it is trained have a significant impact on the performance of the solution, so it is crucial to carefully consider these aspects of the AI project. The training process involves adjusting the model's parameters to minimize the error, hyperparameter tuning, preventing overfitting, and using ensemble learning techniques to improve the performance of the model.

Evaluation and improvement

Developing AI solutions is a complex process that requires careful evaluation and improvement. It is important to regularly assess the performance of AI algorithms and make adjustments as needed to ensure that they continue to meet the needs of their intended users. In this article, we will discuss some of the key considerations and best practices for evaluating and improving AI solutions.

Evaluation

Evaluating AI solutions is a critical step in the development process. It is important to understand how well the AI algorithm is performing and what areas need improvement. There are several different metrics that can be used to evaluate AI solutions, including accuracy, precision, recall, and F1 score.

Accuracy measures the overall accuracy of the AI algorithm and is calculated as the number of correct predictions divided by the total number of predictions. Precision measures the proportion of positive predictions that are actually correct, while recall measures the proportion of actual positive cases that were correctly identified. The F1 score is a weighted average of precision and recall, and is often used as a single metric to evaluate the performance of AI algorithms.

To accurately evaluate AI solutions, it is important to use appropriate datasets. The datasets should be diverse and representative of the real-world situations that the AI algorithm will encounter. Additionally, it is important to split the datasets into training, validation, and testing sets, as this will allow you to evaluate the performance of the AI algorithm in different scenarios.

Improvement

Once the AI solution has been evaluated, the next step is to make improvements. There are several different approaches that can be taken to improve the performance of AI algorithms, including the following:

Feature engineering: One of the key considerations for improving AI algorithms is to carefully engineer the features that are used as inputs to the algorithm. Feature engineering involves selecting the most relevant and informative features, and transforming the data into a format that can be easily processed by the algorithm.

Hyperparameter tuning: Hyperparameters are parameters that are not learned from the data and must be set prior to training the AI algorithm. Hyperparameter tuning involves adjusting these parameters to optimize the performance of the algorithm.

Model selection: Different AI algorithms may perform better or worse on different datasets, depending on the complexity of the problem and the structure of the data. Model selection involves choosing the most appropriate AI algorithm for a given problem.

Ensemble methods: Ensemble methods involve combining multiple AI algorithms to produce a single prediction. This can improve the performance of the AI algorithm by combining the strengths of multiple models.

Data augmentation: Data augmentation involves artificially increasing the size of the dataset by creating new, synthetic samples. This can help to improve the performance of AI algorithms by reducing overfitting and increasing the robustness of the model.

Conclusion

Developing AI solutions is a complex process that requires careful evaluation and improvement. Regularly evaluating the performance of AI algorithms and making adjustments as needed is critical to ensure that they continue to meet the needs of their intended users. By using appropriate evaluation metrics, feature engineering, hyperparameter tuning, model selection, ensemble methods, and data augmentation, you can improve the performance of your AI solutions and achieve better results.

Deployment and maintenance

Deployment and maintenance are crucial steps in the development of AI solutions. Once an AI algorithm has been developed and tested, it must be deployed in a production environment and maintained over time to ensure that it continues to perform as intended. In this article, we will discuss some of the key considerations and best practices for deploying and maintaining AI solutions.

Deployment

Deployment is the process of integrating the AI algorithm into a production environment and making it available for use. There are several different approaches that can be taken to deploy AI solutions, including the following:

On-premise deployment: On-premise deployment involves installing the AI algorithm on a server within your organization's IT infrastructure. This approach provides more control over the deployment environment and can be more secure, but also requires more resources to manage and maintain.

Cloud deployment: Cloud deployment involves using a cloud service provider to host the AI algorithm. This approach is more flexible and scalable, but may involve a trade-off in terms of security and control over the deployment environment.

Edge deployment: Edge deployment involves deploying the AI algorithm on devices at the edge of the network, such as IoT devices or mobile devices. This approach is well suited to AI applications that require real-time processing and low latency, but may also involve challenges in terms of security and maintenance.

Regardless of the deployment approach, it is important to consider the following factors when deploying AI solutions:

Performance: The AI algorithm must perform well in the production environment, providing accurate and timely results.

Scalability: The AI algorithm must be able to handle an increasing volume of data and requests as usage grows over time.

Security: The AI algorithm and its deployment environment must be secure, protecting against potential security threats and data breaches.

Integration: The AI algorithm must integrate smoothly with existing systems and processes, allowing for seamless integration into the production environment.

Maintenance

Maintenance is the process of keeping the AI algorithm up-to-date and functioning as intended over time. Maintenance involves several key tasks, including the following:

Monitoring: Regularly monitoring the performance of the AI algorithm and identifying any potential issues or errors.

Updating: Updating the AI algorithm to address any issues or to incorporate new features and functionality.

Retraining: Retraining the AI algorithm as necessary to ensure that it continues to perform well in light of changing conditions and evolving data.

Debugging: Debugging the AI algorithm to identify and resolve any issues that arise.

Documentation: Keeping accurate and up-to-date documentation of the AI algorithm and its deployment environment, to facilitate ongoing maintenance and support.

Conclusion

Deployment and maintenance are crucial steps in the development of AI solutions. Proper deployment and maintenance of AI algorithms can help to ensure that they continue to perform as intended and meet the needs of their intended users. By considering performance, scalability, security, and integration when deploying AI solutions and monitoring, updating, retraining, debugging, and documenting them over time, you can ensure that your AI solutions continue to provide accurate and reliable results.

IV

Ethical and Social Implications of AI

Bias and fairness

Bias and fairness are important ethical and social considerations in the development and deployment of AI systems. Bias can occur when an AI algorithm is trained on data that is not representative of the population it is intended to serve, leading to unfair or discriminatory outcomes. Fairness, on the other hand, refers to the idea that AI algorithms should treat all individuals equally and provide equal opportunities, regardless of their race, gender, or other personal characteristics.

In this article, we will discuss some of the key issues related to bias and fairness in AI and provide recommendations for addressing these issues.

Sources of Bias in AI

Bias in AI can arise from a number of different sources, including the following:

Data bias: Data bias occurs when the data used to train an AI algorithm is not representative of the population it is intended to serve. For example, if an AI algorithm is trained on data that contains mostly male faces, it may not perform well on female faces.

Algorithm bias: Algorithm bias can occur when the design of the AI algorithm itself introduces bias into the system. For example, an algorithm may be biased against certain groups if it is designed to prioritize certain outcomes over others.

Human bias: Human bias can also play a role in the development and deployment of AI systems. For example, if a human programmer has a preconceived notion about a certain group of individuals, they may inadvertently introduce bias into the AI algorithm they develop.

Addressing Bias and Fairness in AI

To address bias and fairness in AI, it is important to consider the following steps:

Audit and evaluate: Regularly audit and evaluate the performance of AI algorithms to identify potential sources of bias and unfairness.

Diversify data: Use a diverse range of data to train AI algorithms, to ensure that they are representative of the population they are intended to serve.

Transparent algorithms: Develop algorithms that are transparent and explainable, allowing for ongoing evaluation and monitoring of their performance.

Encourage diversity: Foster a diverse and inclusive workplace culture, to ensure that a wide range of perspectives are represented in the development of AI systems.

Establish ethical principles: Establish ethical principles and guidelines for the development and deployment of AI systems, to ensure that they are aligned with the values and goals of the organization.

Continuously monitor and improve: Continuously monitor and improve AI algorithms over time, to ensure that they continue to perform fairly and ethically.

Conclusion

Bias and fairness are important ethical and social considerations in the development and deployment of AI systems. To address these issues, it is important to regularly audit and evaluate AI algorithms, use a diverse range of data, develop transparent algorithms, foster a diverse workplace culture, establish ethical principles, and continuously monitor and improve AI systems over time. By taking these steps, organizations can help to ensure that their AI systems are fair, unbiased, and aligned with the values and goals of the organization.

Privacy and security

Privacy and security are two critical considerations in the development and deployment of AI solutions. AI systems process and store large amounts of sensitive information, making them a prime target for cyber attacks and privacy violations. In this article, we will discuss some of the key issues related to privacy and security in AI and provide recommendations for addressing these issues.

Sources of Privacy and Security Risks in AI

Privacy and security risks in AI can arise from a number of different sources, including the following:

Data breaches: Data breaches can occur when an AI system is hacked or when sensitive information is accessed without proper authorization.

Data misuse: Data misuse can occur when AI algorithms are used to process sensitive information in a way that violates privacy regulations or ethical principles.

Algorithm vulnerabilities: Algorithm vulnerabilities can arise from security flaws in the design or implementation of an AI system, making it susceptible to cyber attacks.

Human error: Human error can also play a role in privacy and security breaches in AI systems. For example, an employee may accidentally expose sensitive information or misconfigure an AI system, making it vulnerable to attack.

Addressing Privacy and Security Risks in AI

To address privacy and security risks in AI, it is important to consider the following steps:

Implement security measures: Implement strong security measures, such as encryption and access controls, to protect sensitive information stored in AI systems.

Regularly monitor and audit: Regularly monitor and audit AI systems to detect and prevent privacy violations and security breaches.

Adhere to privacy regulations: Adhere to relevant privacy regulations, such as the General Data Protection Regulation (GDPR) in the European Union, to ensure that sensitive information is processed and stored in a secure and ethical manner.

Develop secure algorithms: Develop algorithms that are secure and immune to cyber attacks, to prevent unauthorized access to sensitive information.

Train employees: Train employees to understand the importance of privacy and security in AI and to follow best practices for preventing privacy violations and security breaches.

Establish ethical principles: Establish ethical principles and guidelines for the development and deployment of AI systems, to ensure that they are aligned with the values and goals of the organization.

Conclusion

Privacy and security are critical considerations in the development and deployment of AI solutions. To address these issues, organizations should implement strong security measures, regularly monitor and audit AI systems, adhere to privacy regulations, develop secure algorithms, train employees, and establish ethical principles. By taking these steps, organizations can help to ensure that their AI systems are secure and protect the privacy of sensitive information.

Job displacement

The development and deployment of AI solutions have the potential to bring significant benefits to society, but they also raise concerns about job displacement. As AI systems become more capable and widespread, they have the potential to automate many jobs that were previously performed by humans. In this article, we will discuss some of the key issues related to job displacement in the age of AI and provide recommendations for addressing these concerns.

Sources of Job Displacement in AI

There are several factors that contribute to job displacement in AI, including the following:

Automation of routine tasks: AI systems are particularly well suited to automate routine tasks, such as data entry and analysis. This can lead to job displacement for workers who were previously employed in these roles.

Advancements in technology: As AI technology continues to advance, it has the potential to automate an increasing number of jobs, including those that were previously considered to be safe from automation.

Economic incentives: Economic incentives also play a role in job displacement in AI. As AI systems become more cost-effective, organizations may choose to replace human workers with AI systems, even if the human workers are more capable in some ways.

Addressing Job Displacement in AI

To address the issue of job displacement in AI, it is important to consider the following steps:

Encourage reskilling and upskilling: Encourage workers to reskill and upskill in order to remain competitive in the age of AI. This can be done by providing training and education programs, as well as by supporting the development of new skills and careers that are well-suited to the age of AI.

Support transition programs: Support transition programs to help workers who are displaced by AI to find new employment opportunities. This can include job placement services, unemployment benefits, and other support programs.

Promote fair labor practices: Promote fair labor practices, such as providing a living wage and fair benefits, to help ensure that workers are protected from the negative impacts of job displacement in AI.

Invest in research and development: Invest in research and development to create new jobs in industries that are well-suited to the age of AI. This can include investment in industries such as renewable energy, biotechnology, and information technology.

Foster collaboration between businesses and communities: Foster collaboration between businesses and communities to create job opportunities in areas affected by job displacement in AI. This can include initiatives such as community development programs, partnerships between businesses and schools, and investment in infrastructure and technology.

Conclusion

Job displacement is a major concern in the age of AI, but it is possible to address this issue by taking a proactive and collaborative approach. By encouraging reskilling and upskilling, supporting transition programs, promoting fair labor practices, investing in research and development, and fostering collaboration between businesses and communities, we can help to ensure that the benefits of AI are shared widely and that workers are protected from the negative impacts of job displacement.

Responsibility and accountability

The development and deployment of AI solutions come with a great deal of responsibility and accountability. AI systems have the potential to impact people's lives in significant ways, and it is important to ensure that these impacts are positive and that the systems are designed and used in a responsible and ethical manner. In this article, we will discuss some of the key issues related to responsibility and accountability in AI and provide recommendations for addressing these concerns.

Sources of Responsibility and Accountability in AI

There are several factors that contribute to the responsibility and accountability in AI, including the following:

Transparency: AI systems can be complex and difficult to understand, making it challenging for people to assess their behavior and outcomes. As a result, it is important to ensure that AI systems are transparent, so that people can understand how they work and why they make certain decisions.

Bias: AI systems can be biased, which can result in unfair and harmful outcomes. Bias can be introduced into AI systems in a variety of ways, including through the data used to train the systems, the algorithms used to develop the systems, and the values and assumptions of the people who develop and use the systems.

Responsibility for outcomes: AI systems can have a significant impact on people's lives, and it is important to ensure that those responsible for these systems are held accountable for their behavior and outcomes.

Addressing Responsibility and Accountability in AI

To address the issue of responsibility and accountability in AI, it is important to consider the following steps:

Ensure transparency: Ensure that AI systems are transparent, so that people can understand how they work and why they make certain decisions. This can be done by providing clear explanations of the systems' behavior, as well as by making the underlying data and algorithms used by the systems available for examination.

Monitor for bias: Monitor for bias in AI systems and address it when it is detected. This can be done by testing AI systems for bias, auditing the data used to train the systems, and considering the values and assumptions of the people who develop and use the systems.

Establish clear lines of responsibility: Establish clear lines of responsibility for AI systems and ensure that those responsible for the systems are held accountable for their behavior and outcomes. This can include providing oversight and regulation of AI systems, as well as holding individuals and organizations accountable for their use of AI.

Foster a culture of ethics: Foster a culture of ethics in the development and use of AI, by promoting ethical considerations in the design and deployment of AI systems. This can include incorporating ethics into the curriculum of AI training programs, promoting ethical considerations in the workplace, and engaging with stakeholders to ensure that the impacts of AI are positive.

Encourage public participation: Encourage public participation in the development and use of AI, by providing opportunities for people to provide feedback, suggest improvements, and hold organizations and individuals accountable for their use of AI.

Conclusion

Responsibility and accountability are important considerations in the development and deployment of AI solutions. To ensure that AI systems are developed and used in a responsible and ethical manner, it is important to ensure transparency, monitor for bias, establish clear lines of responsibility, foster a culture of ethics, and encourage public participation. By taking these steps, we can help to ensure that the impacts of AI are positive and that people are protected from the negative consequences of these systems.

V

Future of AI

Advancements in AI

Advancements in AI technology have revolutionized the way businesses and organizations operate and have the potential to bring about significant benefits for society as a whole. The development of AI solutions has been driven by a combination of advances in data processing and machine learning algorithms, as well as a growing demand for more sophisticated and intelligent systems. In this article, we will examine some of the key advancements in AI and the implications of these advances for the development of AI solutions.

Improved Data Processing Capabilities

One of the key advancements in AI has been the improvement of data processing capabilities, which has enabled the development of more sophisticated and intelligent systems. With the advent of big data, organizations are now able to collect and analyze vast amounts of data to gain new insights and make better decisions. AI systems are able to leverage this data to learn from patterns and relationships, allowing them to make more accurate predictions and recommendations.

Advancements in Machine Learning

Another important advancement in AI has been the development of more advanced machine learning algorithms, which are able to learn from data in real-time and make predictions and recommendations based on that data. These algorithms are designed to be flexible and scalable, allowing them to be adapted to different use cases and deployed at scale.

Increased Automation

Another major advancement in AI has been the increasing automation of many tasks and processes, which has made it possible to reduce human error and increase efficiency. AI systems are now able to automate a range of tasks, from simple repetitive tasks such as data entry to more complex processes like risk management and fraud detection. This increased automation is helping organizations to streamline their operations and focus on their core competencies.

Increased Adoption of AI

The advancements in AI technology have also led to an increase in the adoption of AI solutions by businesses and organizations. This has created a growing demand for skilled AI professionals who can develop and deploy these systems, as well as for companies that specialize in the development of AI solutions. As a result, the AI industry is growing rapidly, and is expected to continue to grow in the coming years.

Implications of Advancements in AI for Developing AI Solutions

The advancements in AI have significant implications for the development of AI solutions, including:

Increased Accuracy and Performance

As AI systems become more sophisticated and intelligent, they are able to deliver more accurate and effective results. This is particularly important in areas such as healthcare, where accurate predictions and recommendations can have a significant impact on patient outcomes.

More Efficient and Cost-Effective Solutions

Advancements in AI technology have also made it possible to develop more efficient and cost-effective solutions. By automating tasks and processes, AI systems can help organizations to reduce their costs and improve their bottom line.

More Robust and Secure Solutions

With the increasing adoption of AI solutions, there is a growing need for systems that are robust and secure. Advancements in AI technology are helping to address these concerns, by making it possible to develop systems that are less susceptible to attack and more secure against data breaches.

Conclusion

Advancements in AI technology have brought about significant benefits for society, including increased accuracy and performance, more efficient and cost-effective solutions, and more robust and secure systems. As the AI industry continues to grow and evolve, it is important to ensure that these advancements are used in a responsible and ethical manner, to bring about positive and sustainable outcomes for society as a whole.

Integration with other technologies

Integration with other technologies is a critical aspect of developing AI solutions that can deliver real value to businesses and organizations. The integration of AI with other technologies such as the Internet of Things (IoT), cloud computing, and blockchain, can help to create more sophisticated and intelligent systems that can transform the way organizations operate. In this article, we will examine the benefits of integrating AI with other technologies, and the implications of these integrations for the development of AI solutions.

Integration with IoT

The Internet of Things (IoT) is a network of devices that are connected to the internet and can communicate with each other. The integration of AI with IoT can create intelligent systems that can automate processes, gather and analyze data in real-time, and make predictions and recommendations based on that data. For example, an AI-powered IoT system can monitor and control a building's energy usage, reducing waste and reducing energy costs.

Integration with Cloud Computing

Cloud computing provides organizations with access to a shared pool of computing resources, including data storage, processing power, and applications. The integration of AI with cloud computing can help to create more sophisticated and scalable systems that can process large amounts of data and make predictions and recommendations based on that data. For example, an AI-powered cloud computing system can analyze data from a variety of sources, including social media, to provide insights into customer behavior and preferences.

Integration with Blockchain

Blockchain is a decentralized ledger that provides secure and transparent record-keeping for digital transactions. The integration of AI with blockchain can create systems that can ensure the integrity and security of data, while also enabling the creation of more intelligent and automated systems. For example, an AI-powered blockchain system can automate the process of supply chain management, reducing the risk of fraud and improving efficiency.

Implications of Integration with Other Technologies for Developing AI Solutions

The integration of AI with other technologies has significant implications for the development of AI solutions, including:

Improved Performance and Accuracy

The integration of AI with other technologies can help to create more sophisticated and intelligent systems that can deliver more accurate and effective results. For example, an AI-powered IoT system can monitor and control a building's energy usage, reducing waste and reducing energy costs.

Increased Scalability

The integration of AI with cloud computing and other technologies can help to create more scalable systems that can process large amounts of data and make predictions and recommendations based on that data. This increased scalability can help organizations to grow and expand their operations, while also reducing costs and improving efficiency.

Improved Security and Privacy

The integration of AI with technologies such as blockchain can help to ensure the security and privacy of data, reducing the risk of data breaches and protecting sensitive information.

Conclusion

The integration of AI with other technologies such as IoT, cloud computing, and blockchain, can help to create more sophisticated and intelligent systems that can deliver real value to businesses and organizations. As the AI industry continues to grow and evolve, it is important to ensure that these integrations are used in a responsible and ethical manner, to bring about positive and sustainable outcomes for society as a whole. The development of AI solutions that are integrated with other technologies can help organizations to streamline their operations, reduce costs, and improve their bottom line, making it an important area for businesses and organizations to focus on.

Challenges and opportunities

Artificial Intelligence (AI) is a rapidly growing field that is transforming the way businesses and organizations operate. While the development of AI solutions offers numerous opportunities for organizations to improve their operations, it also presents a number of challenges that need to be overcome. In this article, we will examine some of the key challenges and opportunities in developing AI solutions.

Technical Challenges

One of the biggest challenges in developing AI solutions is the technical difficulty of creating and implementing AI algorithms that can effectively process and analyze data. AI algorithms require large amounts of data and computing power to function, and the quality of the data used can significantly impact the accuracy of the results. In addition, the complexity of AI algorithms can make them difficult to implement, requiring significant technical expertise and resources.

Data Privacy and Security

The use of AI involves processing large amounts of sensitive data, including personal and financial information, which presents a significant challenge in terms of data privacy and security. Organizations need to ensure that the data they use to train AI algorithms is protected, and that the algorithms themselves are secure against hacking and other forms of cyber-attack.

Bias and Fairness

Another key challenge in developing AI solutions is ensuring that the algorithms are free from bias and unfairness. AI algorithms can learn from the data they are trained on, and if that data is biased, the algorithms themselves can become biased as well. This can result in AI systems that discriminate against certain groups of people, which is a major ethical concern.

Regulation

The development of AI solutions is regulated by a number of laws and regulations, including data protection and privacy laws, as well as laws related to the use of AI in areas such as healthcare and financial services. Ensuring compliance with these regulations can be a significant challenge for organizations developing AI solutions.

Opportunities in Developing AI Solutions

Despite the challenges, the development of AI solutions also presents a number of opportunities for organizations, including:

Increased Efficiency and Productivity

AI solutions can help organizations to automate routine tasks, freeing up employees to focus on higher-value activities. AI systems can also process and analyze large amounts of data in real-time, providing organizations with insights that can help to improve their operations and decision-making.

Improved Customer Experience

AI systems can provide organizations with a deeper understanding of their customers, allowing them to personalize their offerings and improve the customer experience. AI-powered customer service systems can also automate routine tasks, reducing response times and improving customer satisfaction.

New Business Models and Revenue Streams

The development of AI solutions can also create new business models and revenue streams, as organizations use AI to create new products and services. For example, organizations can use AI to develop personalized products and services, such as customized financial advice, which can be sold to customers as a subscription service.

Conclusion

The development of AI solutions presents a number of challenges and opportunities for organizations. While organizations need to overcome technical difficulties and ensure data privacy and security, the development of AI solutions also presents opportunities for increased efficiency and productivity, improved customer experience, and new business models and revenue streams. To maximize the benefits of AI, organizations need to invest in developing solutions that are effective, efficient, and ethically sound. By overcoming the challenges and embracing the opportunities, organizations can unlock the full potential of AI and transform their operations for the better.

VI

Conclusion: Recap of key points

Importance of staying informed and up-to date.

Artificial Intelligence (AI) is a rapidly evolving field that is transforming the way organizations operate. With new AI solutions and technologies emerging all the time, it is essential for organizations developing AI solutions to stay informed and up-to-date with the latest developments in the field. In this article, we will explore the importance of staying informed and up-to-date in developing AI solutions.

Keeping Pace with Advancements
One of the most important reasons for staying informed and up-to-date is to keep pace with advancements in the field. AI is a rapidly evolving field, and new solutions and technologies are being developed all the time. By staying informed and up-to-date, organizations can ensure that they are using the latest technologies and solutions, which can help to improve the accuracy and effectiveness of their AI systems.

Keeping Up with Ethical and Legal Developments

Another important reason for staying informed and up-to-date is to keep up with ethical and legal developments in the field. AI raises a number of ethical and legal concerns, such as data privacy and security, bias and fairness, and the impact of AI on jobs and the workforce. By staying informed and up-to-date with the latest developments in these areas, organizations can ensure that their AI solutions are ethically sound and compliant with relevant laws and regulations.

Avoiding Technical Debt

Developing AI solutions involves a significant investment of time and resources, and organizations need to ensure that their investments are protected. By staying informed and up-to-date, organizations can avoid technical debt, which occurs when an organization invests in a technology or solution that quickly becomes obsolete. By staying informed and up-to-date, organizations can ensure that they are investing in technologies and solutions that will remain relevant and valuable in the future.

Making Better Decisions

Finally, staying informed and up-to-date is essential for making better decisions in developing AI solutions. The AI field is complex, and organizations need to be well-informed about the latest technologies and solutions in order to make informed decisions about how to proceed. By staying informed and up-to-date, organizations can make informed decisions about which technologies and solutions to invest in, and how to develop and implement AI systems that are effective, efficient, and ethically sound.

How to Stay Informed and Up-to-Date

There are many ways to stay informed and up-to-date in developing AI solutions, including:

Attending Conferences and Workshops

Attending conferences and workshops is a great way to stay informed and up-to-date with the latest developments in the AI field. Conferences and workshops provide opportunities to network with other professionals in the field, learn about the latest technologies and solutions, and discuss ethical and legal concerns.

Reading Industry Publications

Reading industry publications, such as journals and magazines, is another effective way to stay informed and up-to-date. Industry publications provide in-depth coverage of the latest technologies and solutions, as well as insights into ethical and legal developments in the field.

Participating in Online Communities

Participating in online communities, such as forums and discussion groups, is another effective way to stay informed and up-to-date. Online communities provide a platform for discussing the latest technologies and solutions, as well as sharing experiences and best practices in developing AI solutions.

Final thoughts and recommendations.

Artificial Intelligence (AI) is transforming the way organizations operate, and the development of AI solutions is a complex and challenging process that requires careful planning and execution. In this article, we have discussed a number of important considerations for developing AI solutions, including ethical and social implications, privacy and security, job displacement, responsibility and accountability, advancements in AI, integration with other technologies, and the importance of staying informed and up-to-date.

With these considerations in mind, here are some final thoughts and recommendations for developing AI solutions:

Focus on Ethical and Social Implications

The development of AI solutions raises a number of ethical and social implications, and it is important for organizations to carefully consider these implications as they develop their AI systems. Organizations should take steps to address concerns about bias and fairness, data privacy and security, and the impact of AI on jobs and the workforce.

Emphasize Privacy and Security

Privacy and security are critical considerations in developing AI solutions, and organizations should take steps to ensure that their AI systems are secure and protect sensitive data. This may involve implementing privacy-enhancing technologies, such as encryption and secure data storage solutions, as well as developing and enforcing policies and procedures that protect data privacy.

Consider the Impact of AI on Jobs and the Workforce

The development of AI solutions has the potential to disrupt the job market and displace workers, and it is important for organizations to consider the potential impacts of AI on the workforce. Organizations should take steps to ensure that their AI solutions are implemented in a way that minimizes the displacement of workers, and that they are working to retrain workers who may be impacted by automation.

Ensure Responsibility and Accountability

The development of AI solutions requires organizations to take responsibility for the impact of their systems on society, and to be accountable for the decisions that they make. Organizations should ensure that their AI systems are designed and implemented in a way that is transparent, fair, and responsible, and that they are held accountable for any negative consequences that may result from their use of AI.

Stay Informed and Up-to-Date

Finally, it is essential for organizations developing AI solutions to stay informed and up-to-date with the latest advancements in the field. Organizations should attend conferences and workshops, read industry publications, and participate in online communities in order to stay informed and up-to-date with the latest developments in AI.

In conclusion, developing AI solutions is a complex and challenging process that requires careful planning and execution. By focusing on ethical and social implications, emphasizing privacy and security, considering the impact of AI on jobs and the workforce, ensuring responsibility and accountability, and staying informed and up-to-date, organizations can develop AI solutions that are effective, efficient, and responsible.

Will artificial intelligence replace humans?

The question of whether artificial intelligence will replace humans is one that has been debated for decades, with opinions ranging from absolute certainty that AI will eventually take over all jobs to the belief that it will never be possible for machines to replace human workers. In this essay, we will explore both sides of this argument and try to answer this question in the most objective way possible.

On the one hand, proponents of AI believe that machines will eventually replace humans in most jobs. They argue that AI is becoming more advanced every day and that it is only a matter of time before it becomes more efficient and effective than humans in many fields. For example, some experts predict that AI will eventually replace doctors, lawyers, and even scientists, as machines become better at analyzing data and making predictions based on that data.

One area where AI is already being used to replace humans is in manufacturing. Many factories around the world have already implemented robotics and other forms of automation to replace human workers in certain tasks. This has led to increased efficiency and productivity, as well as cost savings for companies that no longer have to pay for human labor.

Another argument in favor of AI replacing humans is that machines are not subject to the same limitations as humans. For example, machines do not require breaks, vacations, or sick days. They also do not have the same emotional and psychological needs as humans, which can make them more reliable and consistent in certain tasks.

However, there are also many reasons why AI will not replace humans in the near future. One of the main arguments against AI replacing humans is that machines still lack the creativity, empathy, and critical thinking skills that are essential for many jobs. For example, while machines can analyze data and make predictions based on that data, they are not yet able to understand the nuances of human behavior and emotions in the same way that humans can.

Another argument against AI replacing humans is that machines can only do what they have been programmed to do. They cannot learn new skills or adapt to new situations in the same way that humans can. This means that while machines may be able to perform certain tasks more efficiently than humans, they will always be limited by their programming and cannot replace humans in all fields.

Furthermore, some argue that the use of AI will create new jobs rather than replace existing ones. As AI becomes more prevalent in society, there will be an increased demand for people who can design, program, and maintain these machines. This will create new job opportunities in fields such as engineering, computer science, and data analysis.

In conclusion, while AI is undoubtedly becoming more advanced and efficient every day, it is unlikely that it will replace humans in the near future. While machines may be able to perform certain tasks more efficiently than humans, they lack the creativity, empathy, and critical thinking skills that are essential for many jobs. Additionally, the use of AI is likely to create new job opportunities rather than replace existing ones. As technology continues to advance, it will be important for society to find ways to integrate AI into our lives in a way that benefits both machines and humans.

What artificial intelligence can't do

Artificial Intelligence (AI) has made remarkable strides in recent years, transforming the way we live, work, and interact with technology. AI algorithms and systems are capable of processing massive amounts of data, recognizing patterns, and making predictions with impressive accuracy. However, despite its tremendous progress, AI still has limitations and cannot do everything. In this article, we will discuss some of the things that AI cannot do.

AI cannot replicate human creativity

One of the defining characteristics of human beings is their creativity. Humans are capable of producing original ideas, concepts, and works of art that are not replicable by machines. While AI algorithms can generate outputs based on data, they cannot create something entirely new from scratch.

AI cannot understand emotions

Emotions are a complex and nuanced aspect of human experience that AI cannot fully comprehend. While AI systems can recognize facial expressions, vocal tone, and other physiological indicators of emotions, they lack the ability to empathize with humans and understand the nuances of emotional responses.

AI cannot replace human intuition

Human intuition is a valuable asset in many areas, including decision-making, problem-solving, and innovation. While AI algorithms can analyze vast amounts of data and provide insights, they cannot replace the human intuition that often plays a critical role in making the right decision.

AI cannot replace human interaction

Human interaction is a fundamental aspect of our social and emotional well-being. While AI chatbots and assistants can simulate conversations, they cannot replace the depth and complexity of human interaction, including nonverbal cues, empathy, and social context.

AI cannot understand human culture and context

Culture and context play a significant role in shaping human behavior and attitudes. AI algorithms can analyze data and identify patterns, but they cannot fully understand the complex cultural and social contexts that inform human behavior.

AI cannot replicate human consciousness

Consciousness is a defining characteristic of human beings, and it remains one of the most elusive and mysterious phenomena in science. While AI systems can simulate intelligence, they cannot replicate the subjective experience of consciousness.

AI cannot replace human judgment

Human judgment is often based on experience, intuition, and values that are difficult to quantify and program into AI algorithms. While AI can provide data-driven insights and recommendations, it cannot replace the nuanced and context-specific judgment that humans bring to decision-making.

AI cannot replace human ethics

Ethics is a complex and evolving field that requires human judgment, empathy, and moral reasoning. While AI algorithms can provide objective analysis and recommendations, they lack the capacity to make ethical judgments and consider the social and moral implications of their decisions.

AI cannot replace human accountability

Accountability is an essential aspect of human society, ensuring that individuals and organizations are held responsible for their actions. While AI systems can provide data-driven insights and recommendations, they cannot be held accountable in the same way as humans.

AI cannot replace human purpose and meaning

Purpose and meaning are essential aspects of human experience that go beyond mere productivity or efficiency. While AI can optimize processes and generate outputs, it cannot replace the sense of purpose and meaning that humans derive from their work and relationships.

In conclusion, while AI has made remarkable progress and has tremendous potential, it still has limitations that cannot be overcome by algorithms and systems. Understanding these limitations is crucial for developing responsible and ethical AI applications that enhance human well-being without replacing the essential aspects of human experience.

Dear readers,

I would like to take a moment to express my sincere gratitude to each and every one of you who have taken the time to read my work. Your support and encouragement

have been invaluable to me, and I am deeply grateful for your attention and interest in my writing.

I would also like to acknowledge the hard work and dedication that went into creating this book. From the initial concept and research to the final editing and publishing, this project was a collaboration between many talented individuals. I would like to thank my editors, researchers, and proofreaders for their tireless efforts in ensuring that this book was the best it could be.

I hope that this book has been educational, informative, and entertaining, and that it has provided you with new insights and perspectives on the subject matter. If it has in any way helped you in your personal or professional life, then my goal has been achieved.

Once again, I would like to extend my sincere thanks to you, my readers, for your support and encouragement. I would be honored to continue to share my thoughts and ideas with you in the future.

Sincerely,

Daniel